THE GIRL WITHOUT ARMS

The Girl Without Arms
by Brandon Shimoda

Black Ocean
Boston · New York · Chicago

Black Ocean
P.O. Box 52030
Boston, MA 02205
blackocean.org

ISBN 978-0-9844752-3-0

Library of Congress Cataloging-in-Publication Data

Shimoda, Brandon.
 The girl without arms / Brandon Shimoda. -- 1st ed.
    p. cm.
 ISBN 978-0-9844752-3-0
 I. Title.
 PS3619.H573G57 2011
 811'.6--dc22

                              2010047074

FIRST EDITION

For a moment seems
    the only way

To live, to speak
Out of turn
Of impossibility
Whom
      is actually listening

Stuttering interim forests
      everlasting sounds a forest makes
Uncoupling the will to bear
Through firestorm
      no material partner

A moment collapses speech
There is no way to live
Out of turn of impossibility

Whom
Is actually listening is

Warm flowers in a blank field
        agree
To hate each other
        as only friends—

    the errancy between

                    for a silent time
—a field through which a mistake is made

Unendurably
      colorful

                    rivers
                         have risen
Cathedrals of song and embarrassment. The blood

                    extinguished. Spring   is the representation of
The will to end it all   by abundance

At first
I thought
            is it better dead
Then without thinking
            it is, and only—

A familiar hand reaches forward in thought
The way one thought tears into two
            all in common, touching. To be
Forever changed, death says
                        embrace the light in the skin you know
You want
To be, or rather

Forever

—who
     has bested death

for Lisa

DISQUIET
PART ONE

Will this last for more than a flight of membranes on an egg
Beneath skewerwoods in hell, Wake up

I wake
As one finding favor within soft crisis
A voice in my ear
Arachnid book lung growing a grave along the wall
I climb at a rate
My mind cannot commit to memory

I put your body on
Your weight rushes through me like a glow of tar
Cutting a terminal swath in the sky
Understand me strung
With bruises elect in a rain of wood
A lamentable assembly of liberal laws
For a harrowing self-
Approving populace

I climb through the black lining of the sky
Sag the relapsing throat of night
Without complement. I want
Thousands of people
To die
At once. I want to watch thousands of people
Jump from windows
One hundred stories high
Glutted with pickled eggs and sparkling wine

Out of tinkling windows
Thrown up, Then served
Again, Thrown up
Again
Then served
Again, A platter of eggs
Mirrored splinters of skull
Sparkling wine red as worship

And I want someone to be playing piano
In a restaurant two hundred stories high
Hunched in the lee of a simple song. There is
Someone hiding in the strings, Many someone's
Hiding in the strings, Many
Someone's
Hiding in the soundboard
Many hammers hammering heads, Missing the rush of the world
Velocity closing in
Late to be comprehended, Someone
Deathly afraid—their heart has stopped—whispering
Into the ear
Of someone also deathly afraid. I want to spend my life
With you, I want to spend my life
Inside
An ear what thinks itself
An organ of infinite warmth, Glistening
Branches of prayer
Making branches burn

And I never wanted children, but now
I want children
To drop
Through skeletal netting
Nameless
Into black beds
As like into potters aglow in generous helpings of children

Grant them reprieve, Bend them over the brisk stools of carbon
Let us cheer our occupation
Proudly into sprays of hazel blood
Bacterial bouquets of liquefied nerves
Nations of skin slick with tantrum

And the simple song
Stops—I am stubborn—and the lining of tar
Forms a baleful perimeter
Around the edge
Of the bed—I am stubborn
You are standing before me
I pull you close, Press my nose to your stomach
Slip your underwear down to your feet

Let them starve, Let them
Drown on convulsing pacemakers
Sidewalks of burnt skin
Cocked, Unstable
Ear-shells
Hemorrhaging through the nose

If I am going to watch
People die in mid-air
Accumulating ash before propulsive ceremonies of gas
Before slamming their copy into the earth
If I am to breathe bowels voided mid-air
Congeries of tar flowers
Riveted
To a burning ear at dawn
Give me a sign
Hold my hair
I will yell down the narrows of an hysteric neck
Before the world gathers speed, Equanimity peeking through stirrups
If I am to watch
The people fall, Refract first spooks of light
Spinning through tar on the ceiling
I might as well start
With my children

WITHOUT RESERVE THERE IS NO LOVE
OPPOSITION A GLORIOUS GIFT

Return to the year broken free

             of breath and heat
In place of a life once considered

Damned   Return to the year
Broken free
             insidious heat
      and harvest

Softly I bite into the stone fruit of human ruin

          freezing my tongue
I graze

All tastes of the stone fruit of human ruin
A pomegranate breaking on a foot
        bridge of freshly laundered skulls
          etymologically strong-
Hold in the air of beheading

            tastes at all   as I want
To taste
A stone fruit of human ruin   wipes
      plasma
        off the cross

The being of a reject is
　　　　the remnants not of love
But essence
　　　　　　by omission
　　　exemplary
Courage of reckless confession
　　　　there is
No tradition beginning
Contrary to deliberating
　　　　guns never miss the target
Thinking
　　　　by love. Thinking love returns

Return to the year broken free
        of negligible survival
My name a nagging emetic

Outpacing the howling unease
        in the sheets

I end each day in the arms of a python
            breathing loudly its scales
Through the mattress   baby nazareth
        trollops
                    the market
Tramples those who cannot
Love   as blades
Slice the air   flesh juices flesh
Drums armored fruit
            as a gift   you promise to spread

To say we will be hungry
For a few months just
Might return us to our bonny forms
The grand days of the Occident
Bent at the windows in our underwear
        in fact no stranger
        to any
        of the figures you made
             me watch. Who knew
A leg could bend
Around the come-on of an axe
        like that

        ... bad faith
Responses to ingenuous questions

We walk
The waterworks. Pet the rabid
        lambs we lamb. The fatherland of hell

The things we want
        to leave the works
The fire in unique denominations
        between
Caress and devotion
        is why I want
To remove myself
Deal only in delicious joy
Freed from myself is success

I felt your hair in the morning
Lift, I wanted to collapse a petal
On—morning
Stretched across the sheet, moldable on
My sleeve, I wanted to make
You visible among the torches
Blow the barbs off the pinked silk of your
Head, then lift, then
Descend, a perfectly pulled diamond down the path through
The desert. Scalp
Scorched through an eye aftermath

Stalagmites flag the desiccated lake
Set wide above torn cheeks

That kind of god would be sitting on my legs in a shaded stone house
Distracted when I kiss your spine
That kind of god loves the way we look in
A mirror of taciturn stone approves
The way we look
In the swift shield of each other's shoulder
Blades pulsing wreckage through the principle of that kind of
God draws a bath
Beneath the sun. A little shrine
Around a waning flame
Your face the screen of a little shrine

In the blown open bay of a little shrine
Patient and curdled, you asked me
How the interview went. This was in fact the interview

I had no answer to reconcile the past tense with
The present, so I
Shut up—
        the down-turn of your mouth
Questions rent from a wet cocoon

Either revised tear sheets of insurgent poems between your cheeks
Or beads from paper arms pried loose as a curtain torn across your hips
Black clouds
Piqued
Bush the shore
Vegetation is shore custard skin

Your hair lifted off. A slant eye
Grooved a password along the floor
That kind of god that clothes itself in energy and specifically flammable leaves
The hatred to wrest
From imagination. A slant eye forms a soft mound
Hair threading its tart iris
A wet tongue up the drain like a tombstone
Pull out and press to my face. In my mouth

I will pull you out of my mouth
Split you in the desert
Train the totality of light to bleed the gracious basket broken and grow
A first of you
Fraught mountain sweeping the motions of a squashed plum blossom spring
Until sense dies out you taste

Someone is reading the verse of the muck
Volubly on the delivery bed
Tearing shadows from the swollen boil of the river. I will never see
My friends again, nor feel
The green canary race the penultimate weather of their words
Worried from the corpse, concealed among forty-nine idols
Pronouncing the sacred the processual
Out of the market of "friends"
Flapping over tight grills

I will never see my friends again, theoretically, these are
Our friends, carrying through
The intimacy of words
Wild plume a disheartening ghetto. I will never
See the images again, carrying through the vacuum of words
Light where soft, where wild and soft
Light dresses into words, as permissions cannot untie
From death
Is the gesture of legacy

GHETTO
Mouths and masters
Thrust no kindness nor kind direction
Until we climb inside betrayal I bring
A gun to our hands
You are clean, I am cleaning
Swollen with a hand of hardboiled eggs
A kissing bug bites the organic wand
Called forth from the shell from the sac

The prisoner remembers
each of the eggplants   of Fuji—

Inflating insurrectionist colors
        through drought
And in olympian agony
In heaven   holding
        your hand

Through the desert
Emitting a light   holding
Your eye in midnight study

        flatworm eggs a cake as globes
The kissing bug   returns
Into the rows of plants
        you said
                I hate your fucking guts

                I have had no choice
but to dig innumerable holes in the yard
in which to plant the babe in arms
        infirms. My stomach drops

What are you putting in the holes
          or pulling
The aroma of the garden   out
          in other words
In other
          descanted eve of rooms   we yell
What else   to do
          the garden grieve   The eggplant
Drags   the stalk

                though I did not cry
And then I cried

                a plague of clouds

                riverbank showered with corneas
                rising
                the sonic ring of trees

                in the silence
Hovers the jaw
Elisabeth and Lucas, I am sorry

I recognize the back of your head
From your poems

You are walking towards something other than
The stylizations of a technical image

Many matches of blood to be scanned
To render the crisis of particular thought

Perspicuous bullets, fire, a target
Flattened against a cactus, riddled
With affection
Looking back at you looking directly

I have taken a liking to bullets
Fast in the bulk of a struggling form

---

        an archipelago of severed breasts
Expressing heavy metals
Disinterred from brideyard silt, dowsing brideful milk

A bullet splits apart an eye
Intent upon its prey

In sleep you dream across from me
You sit on me you gasp on me
Your breath webs lanterns in coverings
Your breast shine why is washing up carcasses
Rubbing fire from bells in monument dark

Shadows dissolve up the side of your shirt
Ribs freezing the world perpetually destroys
Around us if you do not get up
The moment before you lose your slip
I read from the cut in the mirror

IT IS
        I WHO

SAW WHAT I SHOULD
               HAVE NOT

             FOXES SOLEMN
                  IN VEILS AND ROBES
         DRAGGED THROUGH THE RECEIVING FOREST

BURNING GUTS FLYING OVER THE GATE

            I WANTED TO BUY YOU A GIFT

      SO A KNIFE
             INSCRIBED WITH THE PORTENT OF YOUR

   HEART   LOVES REBELLING
                SOON

FROM MYTHISTOREMA

From our left the south wind blows and drives us mad
                          strips bones of their flesh
Our house among pines

    writing   the letters we've been writing
   many months now, dropping them
Into the space between us in order to fill it

             you lowered your eyes
        sweeter than oil
On a wound, more joyful than   water
To the palate, more peaceful than a swan's wings

At night if we remain in front of the white wall
Your voice approaches   like the hope of fire
    again this wind hones

Each of us writes   the same thing
    each falls silent in the other's presence
Watching, each of us, the same world separately

          a heavy rain and again today
The covered sky burdens   Our thoughts
          yesterday's downpour
Bunched up and useless
Would build a collapsing tower

         open to the sound wind
With the mountain   in front of us hiding you
Who will appraise   us the sentence to oblivion
Who will accept our offering

THE AIR THAT STUNS PREDICTS
Intermittently
Harm

The command of possibility
I have been thinking ...

That I have been thinking
Despite regiments of thongs whipping the air of indolent practice
Conveyed down a procession of militant hands
Apocrypha moved to permit a world-reconfiguring jealousy
Overhanging the street in fastness and less distribution
Your necklace flying off in a torrid unit of sweat
Compelled to hack, if not to kill
The clot of angels
Deaf
In moving vales of variable thinking
Lodged in an egg so morose

The imprint of a "tender coffin" on a "giant" tendon
Sequence climbed into without comment

        split
Sanctuary of grief

       stingtongue
               remembrance   in remembrance

Falling out of immediate view
Bombs the consistency of plums
Opaque menagerie   throbbing

               ... about casualties

About waking up among casualties
About the bitter chance of waking up among casualties
About waking up surrounded by wooden sprites in a crib
Surrounded by eleven or twelve siblings
Bled into sheets, lumped in the unbearable manner of hoecake

About bitter chance
Is what a casualty is
Engrailed
To what
Do I owe the distaste
What do I fancy the transfer of chance
From one who looks like me, and yet
Patterned after all the rest, slack beyond the state

You spoke directly into my ear
Pulled at the lonely yellow horses in the dirt
Halos of error within arcs of reaction
As the next thing—Take me to the silver bow—Forget
The wall
Removed for the flood
Built back to the opposite ground
Releases naturally

Casualties are my thinking
Circling unto a spiral at the center of which
And at the edges of which
The center and the edges erupt into a palace without breasts

One eye on the moon
One hand on the heart
Hanging every glance, every compass of deep attention
Every sketch upon the opposite hill
Every momentary pause
In every transubstantiation of attention into worship
Acts of misdirected worship, removing ourselves into the far fields
Writ modestly on the air
In every pause, in every stretch
Beyond the border
Unfolds an ornamental fan

THROUGH EVERY GOD
IS AN EMPRESS OATH BEFORE THE BOMBS
SACRED YOU
AND ME
AWAY
DEVOTED SCORES
A BOMB IS AN OATH WHAT POWER MADE
IN SACRED STRIPS FROM FACE AND CHEST
SKINNED MY GOD IS AN EMPRESS OATH
FLESH UNDERNEATH
RED BLACK
RIDGES OF CHARRED NOSE EYES
UTTERED QUEER
BEYOND SCREAMING
IN THE STUTTERING
FOREST
CARRYING A DEAD BABY UPSIDE DOWN
AT MIDNIGHT
IN THE MORNING I LOOKED
UPON THE LIGHT
MY GOD IS AN EMPRESS OATH
WITHOUT NAME I AM
DEVOTED TO YOU
AS YOU ARE THE FORM TAKING US IN ITS ARMS
I BEG WHATSOEVER FOR YOU
TO EMERGE
WITH THE FLASH
AS LIFE IS AN EMPRESS OATH
I SHALL
LOVE DEATH AS WELL

THE GIRL
WITHOUT ARMS

'This once-upon-a-time when seasons failed, and time stared through the wall nor made to leap across, is the hour, the season, seasons, year and years, no wall and wall, where when and when the classic lie dissolves and nakedly time salted is with truth's sweet flood nor yet to mix with, but be salted tidal-sweet—O sacramental ultimate by which shall time be old-renewed nor yet another season move.'

For Elisabeth

Wind off still water. Night mill of the lantern
Where light can reach
New growth. Speech drowns
Perfectly

Just
You. No
One to catch in the moosehorn

Every agonistic blow
Across the inlet
I am that schizophrenic
Plow under razor flowers
Where nothing is ever a thought
Grows supreme
Threading a stanza to climb into
The inlet
Bright slender legs populate
Ovoid stanzas
Hot and spacious as a convent on stilts
Between victim and rapacious victim

The stanza tosses over phantom trees
Goose tongues hollying out like cloched fruit
Among deadstock
Mist has head and groundcover. Red
Flowers knocking green mud to the knee
Rain to the skull
Incessant mugging after
All
Dead out
I do not touch
The water nor meters in fog
On the rocks

Boats stick to our elbows
The cabin goes up
In rhubarb. Rhubarb
Washes over—
The boats
Do not move. There are no people
Like it

I SHOULD BE TELLING YOU ABOUT MAINE. I AM LEAVING SOON
Before fog hardens our veins
The remotest chance a farm might form in the silence between

Do you want to hear about Maine? Of course I want to hear about Maine
I spent last night on the water. Phosphorescence
Eloped the currents
Felt everywhere. Walking up the land, every time I took a step
The seaweed lit from my feet is Elisabeth

For Molly

Walking out to the water
Is more than walking to an ocean of repetitive pardon
A receptive sky bending to lick a school of lavender
Stonecrop necks in the cold of a lone
Inversion, the enormity
Within walking
Together—it is not romantic
And herein lies the problem
With water and rocks
Magnanimous sky when the islands sink
A burning dirge, and thinking about
Oceanic rocks
Cloud tongue wetting the school of ice plants
Mute water and moss and tight water and rocks
Lapping the bones through the skin

Beams of color broken in two
Ocher and a precipitous garden
Your mind keeps literally afloat
A map as an instrument of the sun
Inside your poems your mouth
Withdraws a path of calendars wild
Overbearing the water
Until the shutters fall off the imploded house
Cliff-edge until your brain fans out
Fivefold. How will you write otherwise?
Mussels salivating little bridges in clapping

Forms loose in unaccompanied dawn?
How could you sleep as one and one?
With a seat thrust out of the rock
At the sea
You will always be held to the exilic grain
Sweeping the caps in their patterns of white
Is my problem, I know. You have only begun—

WHO MOST OR LEAST LOVES US AS WE DANGLE
With whom are we willing to cumber
The night makes a house
How much better than one can engage only half-nakedly by day
    the obscurity of the other
In the white grave of hospitality

Bodies cast in milk
Decomposing between cushions
Watch the fly plead with the pitcher plant on the sill
Getting close pulling away leaving for two years coming back
It is me it is us we were young we boiled blood
Faded wings distended thorax of a postulant among fractured roses
Call into my wing flashing convexities

How often does the telephone ring how many rings does it take
To determine which of your former partners is on the other end
Which mountain did they fall from. How loose
Golden cobbles
How many dried fruits in your cheeks
When they fell, how far could you see
Into the distance
And why were you eating dried fruits was there not any bread any bacon

Do the features of a house recharge themselves in reports
Submitted to the emperor—a little bar of cream-white soap
Reducing across the polished floor in its idyll. Nights' injections
Civilians sitting and watching for the lights in the window to flame

I feel the grand efflux of something dark and only partially improved
By the darkness every time someone sits at a piano I think of 1986
—I hated 1986—every night spent kneeling among the sweats in the closet
The twittering of bats in obedient order to the higher lights
Shining between slats from startled sleep
Distance spread across breakfast dough
Fruit powder honey backside tartlet spooks
Licking the necks of white swans

I can feel the breath of one sitting across the legs from me
Thighs with how many seconds of skin
The moment I arrive at home throw open the door
Everything will look the same though earned and how can I slap
    such an angry rump
I am home I say I am home I say and even if the garden has gone
White with guano from the bombs—I have walked the river of three
    roads of ash
I have walked and waited I have bargained for you with the bull of my life
That you might be exactly the only way out

TREES PRODUCE ELEPHANTS TO THE SKY
One assumption among thousands made up with the distance
Opening onto precipitous fields
Parceled by cloud law and shadow
Wringing three girls and one boy between trees
And field spurge
Sweat et cetera
Waters known and unknown both et cetera et cetera

There are marvelous things going on in North Carolina the suffocation
The prating of the miserable past in the hogs' falling off
Flowers at the whirling table of dump river music
I did not know how thoroughly I had been penetrated until I felt
    the intestine resonating
Immediately my body across the table touched the shoulders of her
He was sleeping face down in a meat-endless storm of grain and kudzu crickets

I sat in a small world watching everything gather the raveling
Elephants gathering the wood larger and closer to the leader like a totem
    unraveling
On the night of the twenty-first the four of us drove to the top of the hill
To drink each other's dresses between the trees
The field sousing brown
Those we purchase our transient lives from we fund though does that make
    much sense?
It is beautiful they trumpet they have no use for you are impossible to talk to

Around the eye skin is folded in innumerable waves
Gathering the solar event into edible fat and hot growing over
And dark
Accommodating a moist intractable stare I stand
Between the trees and the field I yearn principally for
The naked eye
A sty of concern in which I realize I am nowhere in particular
What I want to see—floating in on sight or stampeding the skin back
Into the earth—continues to reveal itself as such lustrous ivory through tension

SEVEN SATELLITES OF THE MOON
Alight into our neighborhood
Lick the steeples from balls to prayer
Upon the shanty dwellings

Intentions of dwellings to buildings are buildings for fires
Neighbors slink thirstily to

You love them you clear blankets for them
Fill the space with grapes and massage
Fancy the reverent bobbing wish the consecratory light of the cross

Seven satellites circle Niagara
Men planted women wearing the lot of their plants skinned children
Around their waists, Goodbye, Goodbye
To indigenous facts
Squash blossoms fallen to the floor
I.e. punishment sublimated into employ blossoms make welcoming slaughter

Several bleaches in the aerial shots of you and I
Wedged into the voluminous gears of the grocery
A small horse ascending iron clouds is a fragile gas
Rippling the face of instructive evening
Sit down it is early come on there is nothing to see

Late at night I wake up I stand before the leaded glass the ironing board
Upon which plants have been judiciously arranged
I touch the wandering Jew I touch the jade I touch

The great and dying house suffused with a colicky light
The shades of disquiet look back at you flat in the sheets
Protect me, Depend on me moon damp apostrophe

For Lucas

EXHAUSTED VIRGIN OF THE ALPS
Men smothering the horizon with flags
Sleep beneath an impending tree

Massaging
The sun, Denise Levertov
Buried one hundred yards away from us
At all times poisonous
Gas clouding baby radishes, white cucumbers
Activist blossoms enfolded in corn
Pretending to be dead. We are dead
Unless we do something
Soon—The beautiful gap between your teeth
Will surely persist
As your hair in a pile of apocalypse flame

Red-Red Pride
Lettuce whorled womb
Sustains all helpless chard sexual
Purple
Until the ass falls head over

I ate a panini. I was not impressed
No one is alive who made this the object of their body, I said
Nor could anyone complacently white
As a mess of napkins in a nun's lap

Cars passed in new camouflage
Rent with babies and puppies, parrots of the present

EXHAUSTED VIRGIN OF THE ALPS
Colonial men smothering the horizon with flags
Go to sleep beneath an impending tree
As a black body massaging the sun
Brandon promising entrance to a life away from standard injunctions
Outside bath factories of wood
Loving lines too much to seek their sources in air, exhausted virgin of the Alps
Translated by there are no dead in America
Echo of light that bleeds over no dead in America's there are no dead in
    America
Unconscionable peroxide propaganda longs for
Enchantment
Design and patents that
Never was
Nothing has ever been; the human has everything
Hope is a grave thing. To say farewell and become the farewell
That is fitting
Love is refusing to share

Books collapse teats of private thinking—
Disembodied, half-erect, awaiting orders to land on the table
Ham gruyere havarti and a pickle
Root beer and a salad, root beer turkey chips
Soda brownie and a glass of milk
I ducked beneath the awning at noon
Was met with the pleasant beans of DOING
Spread upon roll halves
Pressed with avocadoes and pork

I bought EXHAUSTED VIRGIN OF THE ALPS
Read aloud to Lucas on our way to the peninsula
Passage us green
White turkey feathers on water
Ribbed into clouds. A small island
Egret in shadow
Larger island. Mammals on a flotilla of wooden combs
Straight and black
Paying fountains to cloud loft
The dark shore
A stripe of snow-to-fall, wind blowing
Lucas bought a book what had been real in words
Began to be replaced
By what was not real, by the not exactly
Real
I am at the part again where Babylon had once been a golden cup in the
Lord's hand, making all the earth drunken but suddenly She is broken is
the Black Sheep Potato Farmer and gleaming white embers of babel down
streets no longer streets

'The other day, in the middle of January, as I was taking a walk in Elizabeth Park, in Hartford, I saw at a little distance across the snow a group of automobiles that had pulled up on one side of the road. A dozen people or more got out of them. They took off their coats and threw them together in a pile on the asphalt. It was then possible to see that this was a wedding party. Often in the summer, particularly on Saturday mornings, one sees such parties there. They come to have photographs taken in the gardens. But these people had come in January. The bride stood up in white satin covered with a veil. An ornament in her hair caught the sunlight and sparkled brightly in the cold wind. The bridesmaids were dressed in dark crimson with low necks. They carried armfuls of chrysanthemums. One of the men stood in the snow taking pictures of the bride, then of the bride surrounded by the bridesmaids, and so on, until nothing more was possible. Now, this bride with her gauze and glitter was the genius of poetry. The only thing wrong with her was that she was out of place.'

Then we were writing a poem for Greta
The body that was once here
Is parting its throat, we have to do something
We have to refuse to suffer an ending

Pull down the lines. We are flat on our backs
Grass dark. Pull down
The paragraphs
Crossing the sky. Pull down the constructions
Our curiosity, it seems
Dissipating into action
However sublimated a compulsion
Prior to any attempt to get along with the dead
Understand exactly what they are doing
What
They are doing, in their own incomparable way
Is correspondence
To exist, documented or woven into poems
Simply the stay against aggression and loneliness
Discovered in stadia of beautiful works of an inexplicable force
Spreading rapidly the atmosphere
Would ever make sense, but we gawk
The tears of a sparrow
For us if it did, estranged from the act of getting close
To the things the people who complicate our existence
Make it the trouble it is
Joy is the harm. Death is its own kind of vegetable farm

For Kelly

I want to remember, No
I want to see
But for the trees transporting us
Immediately through
The depths of their woods
And our woods
The house and our house
Like a clearing of fence
And our fence
Gathered as mist
Cold pastoral armament

Home, then
If I could
Remember any thing of days
Softly taught
With sliding beads of death
As there is no creator like you
Must create
The order to disorder
Against
            you remember?
The fact of our rising
Beating the wires of dust and drawing
To ritualize
Creative calculations of darkness
Wanting after the ghost

Replicating in the images we seek to dispel
Between witness and event
The forge of scar and hunger
And laughter
Corporeal in order
To be believed
Twin bodies entranced by bonfires affections

The shade just might kill us
Justly make us prolific

Do you promise at least the division of risk
Sunk in the house
Of dispassion
Is passion, Polished laser of an elder
Toddling the family syllabary
Thighs slapping wet with ice cream

Dead relatives reach into the cupboard
Shattering reliquary oak
To find a female embedded still
Awaiting her groom
In silence, Blasted
From scalp to neck
Face relocated
To the fry of her palm

Devout awareness is illegal
Dropping to our knees as annuals of ice
Through the feedlot
Whining for what on a warm afternoon
Sunshine defoliating the moon
In the yard
Yet mountain laurel crowds
As we plant with our feet, Our minds
For the moment
Each coming day
Upon the ground
Unrecognizable flags
Harvest volumes of who did not bother
To show
Despite the occasion
There is no turbulence absolute as turbulent love
As the dawning of hate

Where is Father? We never really had
A child we had a child
We never

Really? Had he
Been an expensive Indian
He would have sat
Among chocolate and goose eggs

As he was white
Half starving, Surrounded by chocolate
And beef and goose eggs

Radiant error will never cease
To glow
Cuddlesome
Deer mocking deer
In black triplets, Conceive
The evolving limit of vision
And speech as in, Where
Do they go do we go
What is the source of the cry, Do we go
Where do we go where we stand
Anomic and stuttering
Life nor in death nor in parting

Hunted
By the wick of fat love
In the desert encased in the thought of what
Might kill if he belatedly opens his mouth
Wide to which emission rocks
Listen, The family with dysfunctional charms
Listens, The grass listens
Lights listen, Bottles fallen from the hands of lunatic
Brothers listen, To the hands
Listen, Wombs
In the desert
Listen, Listen
To the picture you prayed for the power
Listens, I am listening, Listen

DISQUIET
PART TWO

OCCASION OF THE MASSIVE

To eat your partner to the brain
And be suffocated by the impossibility that the terrifyingly inert mass of
    wet coral is what loves you
Is to fear
What makes you continue pulling the rest of your partner's organs
Out
With your teeth
In spite of the original desire to barter breath

For a body
Goes out, rank and contrived
Equally to those now living
As dead hands tied to feet, striking the figure of a temple bounding
    wall to wall
To lump of sun in a pocket of air
Fattening upon first mesmerization of freedom
Permitting cannibalisms are of or equals what you and or I are leaning towards

The grave
Now slinking the steps of your neck

I am saying
Anguish

Overbearing any specter of land is foreign I fail it is moving
Across the fallow joints there are no saviors
Without genesis
Widening to nerve splintered light
Anything touched
May well reserve its original stance. Becoming bigger
Monsters

Whinnying how it feels to drive feeling into carnal love

Slide to the floor
Separating into spasms
          will

Walk out of a coma, join under a tomb
Jerking a dark pentagon
Indebted to
          a wilderness of brutish forms
Terrorizing, but honestly...

A second round of World
          remaining   wish
I wish
          when I do

FROM THE SEA AND THE SHADOW

It falls

The night falls

the night sky falls

a star, the eyes follow, my

hand falls

It is never enough / I

am hardly ever enough

I go pulverized through narrow streets with paving stones

Let the walls fall, crumble, fall, crush me finally, end it

the eyes / the hands

I will come

It falls

The half-hour would-be wholeness

falls, the year falls, the mirror

destroys itself / that year, a

brilliant, at times quiescent

star will fall

I lie down

the trees are bright with resisting

polished under the rain .   have shed all their leaves

                                   Corridors

of summer stretch out behind me endless

            like memory like

I destroy myself running through open doors

leading through empty rooms

Or there is someone

I shall come through your eyes from the other side, my

                         water, my mirror

I will come into your belly and make it a sea rolling against me

come into you soft as sleep / and be real

SILVER BOW

I picture you in a wife
           beater in black
Pulled over your skin
           without underwire
That no thing listens
           without worrying itself

Is it a lie   I want to work
Would you consider it
Lying

Impoverishment of lights
On a drive-in theater screen
Vanishing fields   Stand

Picturing each other

TEMPERAMENTS OF AIR
Beyond the ignoble mill
                    of poetry—is looking an
            infection made
            impatiently the vocal rose

TENTACLE
                    of a wet attempt
I like to think of
The squid in your arms
Every time you ask me a question
I do not know how to answer
            which is always

SLEEPING WELL INTO
The afternoon without hearing
   seeds break
Through the coffin
     pink
   and blue and dark absolve
   blue brown and light

     little lass in the field
   and fair looks through you
      foreground for a noose

Forming an eye fraying sight of its margins
   rubbing feet in the basin
      warm you untie me for sleep

TIME WAS
We had finally met
Time was the covering of one hundred degrees
In every movement within your country
I open my eyes within

   no clothes no glasses your wet
     hand anointing my head

   bending over
    wet country

Wild forms lack the swollen root
But it is only a vagina, unaccompanied
Cackle in an orchard
Lighting upon your back
Has never so sweat

The orchard grown purposeful
In any way you tell yourself
The most ridiculous things
When you are alone
Tired is how the arroyo rises
To remark the satiating flower on the wall of tin creatures
Fighting in dander and mist
Milkmaids of the desert knocking everything off
Each limb covered in muscle
Each globe flanged with a muscular being
Only a vagina cannot be held
Did I not suffer that I could hold it
As like unease in the ovarium
No I had thought it given like this

You stand at the door awaiting prevailing winds
To clear the orchard of "other energy"
Without inflammation
I was concerned
When you and I take off our shirts
In unison
Are we not embarrassed? How longish does fruit soak in the spice of blood
I want to say maybe I want to stay awake
If you answer a series of questions then cry
I want to stay awake

Will you wear your nourishing yolk
If you do I will too I will faint

With not so much anger
As violence   I do not want

To be filthy
           void myself against the lights
To rectify the problem of distance. I bang
           my head

Waters arch, Can I say "waters"
                          you are living
           permission

You emerge from a room
That is it—that is all that it takes
Primroses strip me from day

If we are
       truly

All light would
Cease
       exteriorizing

The commune of two

Or
       if what will last

I will be with you always like a maggot
Breeds berates the thing it bathes in love
The glow of unrequited love it says so

Confirms through outfits of translucent skin
The splitting brain of one of three fruits turning slowly
An instrument flower rowing itself through brown water
All of three fruits grown on the backside of a broad farm
Hidden travels slowly over coal

DEATH RICTUS IS A DREAM RICTUS

All possible ways to plug the mouth
All possible things with which
To plug
The mouth
Burnt into button ears folded in repose
Drinks the sweat fetching mouths agape

I go to sleep late morning buried
One hundred feet below the ground
Relieve myself into failed and transplanted necks turned out

I go to sleep against the skirts of women
Internations grazing vines beside pools for something to drop of my youth
Girl washing in a porcelain tub
Boy slipping fingers between scales of beady fish
Girl drying beneath the less radiant of two dynamic sodom sun tablets
Boy validating his resemblance to the girl resembles the boy calico garden

I go to sleep to the sound of water dripping from a cold candle hung from
    a black roof
Pouring skin unto each other's flames of laughter rising over apocalypse farm

I go to sleep late morning one hundred feet
Below
You looking into the veins tearing through the heels of your feet
Swinging back
And forth
One hundred feet above

Are the maggot's affections interminable?
Can we make the maggot's affections interminable?
Let us touch each other over the smear of a waterbird across the ground
Neck twisted scarf snap the air
Let us feed the beak a stick of dynamite
Let us shed ourselves into the network of beams; you slice yourself into a
tapering and erectile root rubbed the length of the long face while I watch you
slice yourself into a tapering and erectile root second and third while I watch
There will be one hundred other things going on in the mid-distance
Let us call fifty of them forward
Make making a foolish enterprise
Scorn
Of emptiness
Let us watch the second fifty conform
Into a wailing, white fence, within which an orchard of apple trees
Springs fire against the gathering sea
Numbers make like muscles against actionable sentences
All islands might withdraw
Let us watch the noise raise up the sails
The sea will be complete, unerring in the dark, like a wedding dress
Let us promise to put ourselves to better use than a wedding dress
Let us be worn by death, better than this, a string of soft shells pulled from a
spiral of wet, fallopian ribbon taken into the mouth, opening in the sea, out of
which a waterbird tears from the plague, tiny ringlets of blood and brain prove
awful on the oil of the slow-moving waves, a column of devils shines upward

IN AN ACT OF TERRIBLE VENGEANCE, I LOVE YOU

Improved where first things are killed, I promise
To come bearing the lightest house
Through the plant and breakfast of sweet kills
The view of the garden
Tearing through composted future
Victim I love I watch you fail
To eliminate no matter who or how
It is Spring
And in Spring it is Winter
And in Spring

Anger dispels you
Floods at four o'clock grazing light at five o'clock
Slipped sideways into air
Faces mouthed from the peaks
Red and white fog, I should have stayed put
I would have eaten myself through the fog
For the people slipped to cold revelations
Flayed to water and springs

The grave is now on the wall. The mind divides along an axis
Between the air to light a room
And the fact of being deprived of air
Large, Lace bruises of necking hell
Keep the head above the expanding clot
Becoming morning light
Awake o'clock

To authoritative repetitions
Father in red numbers
Writing through a crystal haze. Father at the wood for drink
Cells down every limb's troubled skin

Exposures of Father in the alcove
With women, So dressed
Horns filled with menses
Partnering the walls with women jeweled along the inner thigh
Of course there was verse
Singing in conflict

Father posing among hateful boys
Who come
To engorge on politics of self-annihilation
Who care for us, As girls who care for boys
Father ascending the station
Of headhunters
Huntresses, Daughters
Sons
And on ...

Because no one ever cared enough
For you
Because you were entirely cared for, Still
Your body will not lift
Imperfections legal and free

By the might of pallbearers
One eating a sandwich in a long driveway
One eating a sandwich

In a long driveway, and also drinking
Drinking, And also watching three deer
At the far end of a long driveway
Drinking from the arch of circumstance
Spirit bulbs, Bones glowing in pools of noses
Soft shanks, Earflaps dressed as news
Stand about the fields and listen

One eating a sandwich with a rifle
Across his lap, Watching three deer at the far end of a long driveway
Touching a black welt in a sling
One buck in a far field, At a dark remove
A dour and piebald suit of wet sky
Classist among the butterfly

Like curtains across the faces of most witherèds
A congregation devotedly loosens the knot of sound reason
From the bangs of the road
Elysium carved into the scales of the paranoid

I have marked the trees
I like to smell
Where
And when they are ruined
By the merciless imprint of faith
Binding to their huts
Applauding delegates of faith

Little children in the fountain of explosive olives, Bronze fish slicing
    against naked legs
Through brush I smell the scars, Buttons against grease
To smell the math, The aftermath, Rose garden of surrender

How we are moving
The river
On both sides
Embalms our movement
Through the landscape
Our best friend's throat
About the head
And eyes, The eyes
The swelling

Is mine, The painting is mine, The painting
Of the willow on the curtain
Thrown into sudden depiction
Characters fading to the breastplate
Where I threw you onto the counter
Elder tree knocking the moldering plants
Over the border—
I no longer believe in the warmth of the state
You will never eat
So long as shocks break the dishes

Between depressions
Is mine, Lifting hay from the miniature farm folding out
A funereal house in the white atlas of Belgium
Began my anger, I swallowed stacks of butter cookies
Swam perfunctorily in a dark lily pond
Dropped my drawers for the lady of the lens
Some day I will be hard for her, For now
I think of her knives
Spreading brown spots on endless sweet cake
Breeches hanging from the line
Transient shadows my arms

Exposed on a slope of bear grass
Narrow waves
Surrender a smoothed over lap
Sweeping the arch of your brows
Mouth caught thrilling
The sea
Forwarding its locks at our knees
Ghouls arising from foam strong as love
So it is yours...

The cricket leaps into gold, There are spools of songs I cannot hear
Your friend sing in the dead
Underground
Who
Better not have been the spectators in our life, Coiled in the holes in the walls
Wove through the sound in the floor
We promised to ditch

If the ice broke in spears
The curtain closed around us
In emergency
Lavishing blood in the sheets
The record spins, Do you want to hear

Or to suffer
Young, Not knowing where to look
Everything was available to you, and so nothing—

An erratic comb of crowns
Colored mammal heads
Floss yellow cups
Bitch of the wind destroying river mummies in flax
Prosaic swelter of life dying for two
Not a poem to live into, Spit up
Through smoke
No songs ever written on quiet alert
Killing land by the roots
Took color from your face, Made a note
Intravenously
Organs of nocturnal stone
A tomb that passes itself off as sound

Don't touch it, Tell me
What did you see? Strangers lining the road
Spinning propellers
Watching her ascend
Holding the blades, Spinning into the air, Smaller, Smaller

All of the plants are dying
Umbellate lips on a star, Exactly
What you will see late at night
Wintering the already dead

I opened the door
Pulled the suffering lady to the street
Put my fist through her mouth and pulled the roots out
Of the ground, Her eyes filled fast
With milk
I wept into the fish in her throat
Swam back through my eyes
Darts stuffed into her carriage, As if green grass had been stewed
Wept
Into the meal of her life

Each chromosome pushed to the bed
Slashing blankets with collagen veils at the windows
Lifting our arms, Poor in the moment
Rattling wind the world naked

The last thing I said I said see you tomorrow
I remember breathing fitful lines against the slump of the river
We are going at one o'clock, Now it is two
We carry death
Between

The garden closes the mission entranced, I rub
My legs, I rub
My legs

To lakes, I rub my thighs to the eels in the lake
Enlarging the enemy
Contingencies of nuclear rays. A friend gutters from a float
Speaks pollen and pink in transformative grain
Runs with me to the waves, Transfixes
One's fear to the child never born
Swum within every stilled leaf
In which the ground is reflected
Opening national stands in the dirt

Sweat from head to thinking head
A sandwich with radish and loin
A sandwich buoyed by the sex of the radish
A long driveway along which women sell eggs
In lavish splashes, Meatballs in scalding silk

The first two blankets fall
From the funeral
To the mattress. I will never be warm
A third deer sweating into your neck
Hoof overhanging the sheet
Not enough to impregnate a mouse
Carried through the streets of the island
In a box, This is your day
Everyone has gathered, Is walking
Charged
By nymphs masked in the blood
Two hundred local monsters, Two hundred angers
Tempest privately for you, In eulogy—

I wanted to say something plain
But I could no more
Than distract myself
From the petal of vomit on the cloth by the beautiful hand
You wanted me to write
I wanted to eat

It is not that you
Are a failure, You said
Mistrusting the youth in delimiting God
By turning away into something more smart, More
Photographic, In fact
No, You
Looking the evils in the foaming mouth
Expectorating a mirror, Who said
The corpse-drenched sky would slit its wrappings
Rain the vegetal body to my feet
If I could be lucky, Or in the right time

The place has never mattered, And neither
Have I

WHAT HAPPENED TO YOU BACK THERE

I as lost I in the elevations
Slipped when red grapes and the blue grapes not sure
If she looks onto the marigold ascension of street's look for another one note palace
Go to Missoula, I suggested
Find things metering the bright valley love it I imagine guessing
Touching yourself the seeing fires at once
I will not be there You have to get out
Ghostly advancing meadow with little trees
Stands of stomachs in the eighth month
Swings made of travel
Running slows like you
Round of pond feather caught in surface ice
As in the boat lowers into the locks My appendages
Numb with lady ore lung elderly collapse
Sing brown river family floats
Thousands of gold leaf and balconies
Anthem rows of children found us War's milk by the arm
Spin the way paper on a cock
In the morning
I can only hear I did not mean to send you home
Find the stud Beat all
Feels differently in the house light of silence
Knocking What have they knocked over
Lights from the sun in a sawyerish grid
Care for the plants
It was clear I wanted to take part

Rain in the whip the house rocks against a lean fence
Slats break skin off lilac
Through window see a struggling form A long arm of wood
Taken to the walls The barracks will

Rip open The future
Will find the body
In memory Stores of poison Heads against the corners
It is a terrible life when in order to love you must destroy the foundations
You are right about the foundations
The tiny are the angels
I know that now Rescue the fibers

She was there from the beginning Met praevia else
Lived through the orders to disorder
By when went your voice
Flutters a suspended shell at the tree entirely in my ear
Not a distance the distance your face from the bark
Children play at eight and a half
Are you going to take care Do we
Now seem that or cold The song how pick
The irregular egg
I devote myself to
And throw it at me walking
Away slowly
Into air Racking opened
I cannot stop the song The music is the continent

A cavernous space Thousands gathered in solitude Heads
Back against heads
An empty canoe now It must exist somewhere
We walked to the shallows Promotions for our friends
The first time understood the tassels of purple
Felt like I had never paid generous enough witness
Though even that is a precondition
We met at the ring knowing you would encounter
Each window a ghost slack painting in rhyme Outside

Houses being put together Juvenile pokeweed though
No smoke in the chimney
Begins with birds are your birds Like that Asking
I fell from the logs The farmer is going to set fire
To the candidate is a joke
He She does not satisfy Which I see dissent with you
First time attention is paid
As if the body for performance Skin slipping

The corpse wakes us
Simultaneously flat on my back
Looking up into the tree house ropes with wings Still colors As we spoke of
My head as though you scattered small colored candies on the floor when I reached
    for the light
Felt each friendship as plasma Gained the necessary weight
Drank two drank six drank eleventh
Pearls with black irises come and go Soft negative spaces
Elevated I called for you across the State Waited through
The air of blue warrior with finger and blue skin arrows Until
Parting dance ferns you arrive into me I need
The soft however far I walked
Always out off fashion with the ark Climb the prong braid
Lifting earth mound patch of soft desert is fur
Flanks all daymies of foxes

In the movable curst of artists Working desperate eggs up their shadows
On molding towards You want to be capable
Given yourself for pleasure
Little mistake brushing long scrawling nominations
Do not can you sit Pour Revise with For me
Eleven then thirteen on the roof watched the steal birds copulate with clouds
Spreading each friend scented intimacy Each

Touching yourself I beg off Nothing but you pulled down

You're lying on your hand A finger is not enough
You say can You see my face into the country without partner
Hairs fall to the tiles maneuverable
Risk in the ribs equatorial Glow
Plentifully running premières of autumn bleaching
I know her I have known You are the slow pile on stricken wheels
You rise To the door It is me talking on both extremes
Dredging target flowers on green heads the outside
Afraid without choice combing lice Underground

In between time hands grow more erratic less common each
Other is the person who sat on our lap Frame a beautiful face
Bad feeling with the Books beside you

The wall moves closer I can feel it as a farm and thaws
Will no doubt grow you have to let it
We are failing each other twice Are we
The whipping wither glacial reservoirs
Fit in the walk along habitual imperia
Into apologetics I witnessed two bird events today
What if I made more room If I tidied My things are every
Where What if I emptied my self
In the compactor Gulls arranging themselves
Tiny faces the end down on flowering spikes Tear No

I can make out a slight smile is white
Someone standing in the opposite side I wouldn't know It tastes good
My back is feeling better
Out the window flew bread to repent
Became the skin on the back of the grand

Just wants in Will do anything to avoid being inert
Toughest The exact patrons Grand Other warned
Braces for the husband between torches I will side with
Everything off Cozy with saccharine
Don't move away from me
These are the melodies we eat by the river
Got in to our bellies The creatures raising flags conquest in gray and rich woods
Rolling hills the craft of living alone with some one and one's colors stretched
        coverings
I thought we were making a life And hitting was
YOU. AM NOT GOING TO PLAY
No more ... I am here The disorders have committed
We cannot quit daily our lives into a new time
Wonder what held the body in The sheets sailed over the field from the falls
Turning blue in the dragon expanse Snapping the body loose
Field of black is not a lake
Your thinking from a distance That we are not strong enough
To set the missing aside and compel
Ourselves to do the interim work of loving from a far
We would be better But when has better
Mattered So we talk through phones of come
Entire lives flashed before
The same songs love songs til the bell shadow swells its blood seed will continue
Please why poetryfuck poetry hate it don't want to do it
When it Comes through L
Is for Labor L is for laceration balm is for you
But no Life is for the flying L
S for B for
I get it You sound to me as you feel entirely broken
Still wet will our mouths open Ever

The Girl Without Arms was written in Missoula and Rock Creek, Montana; Seattle, Washington; and Trescott, Maine

The cover image is a family insignia taken from a photographic portfolio made and belonging to my grandfather, Midori Shimoda (1910-1996)

"From Mythistorema" (p. 28) is an erasure and adaptation of the seventh section of George Seferis' "Mythistorema," Edmund Keeley and Philip Sherrard translation

"I shall love death as well" (p. 33) is a line from the ninety-fifth song of Rabindranath Tagore's Gitanjali

"This once-upon-a-time when seasons failed..." (p. 37) is from Laura Riding's "Poet: A Lying Word"

The poem *"For Lucas"* (p. 50) includes lines from poems by Frank X. Gaspar ("I am at the part again where Babylon had once been a golden cup in the Lord's hand, making all the earth drunken but suddenly She is broken" from "Wail For Her"), Henrietta Goodman ("Black Sheep Potato Farmer" from "Matryoshka") and Matthew Kaler ("gleaming white embers of babel down streets no longer streets" from "On the First Morning Without Sadness"). The passage beginning *"The other day, in the middle of January..."* is from a speech given by Wallace Stevens in acceptance of the Gold Medal from the Poetry Society of America, in 1951. "The body that was once here is parting its throat" is from Greta Wrolstad's poem, "Notched"

"From The Sea and the Shadow" (p. 63) is an erasure and adaptation of Paul Blackburn's "The Sea and the Shadow"

Thank you especially to music and poetry ...

Thank you to the following individuals and publications, for providing homes for some of the poems in this book: Timothy Donnelly, Karen Volkman and *Boston Review*; Adam Robinson and *Everyday Genius*; Sommer Browning, Tony Mancus and Flying Guillotine Press's *Apocalypse Anthology*; Maxine Chernoff, Paul Hoover and *New American Writing*; Sam Lohmann and *Peaches and Bats*; Gillian Conoley and *VOLT*; and Lacey Hunter and *West Wind Review*

My utmost gratitude to Janaka Stucky, Carrie Olivia Adams, and everyone at Black Ocean, for their supreme and fortifying support, vitality and vision; and for their great faith and radical hearts, CAConrad, Dorothea Lasky and Tomaž Šalamun

For their company, generosity and grace throughout the writing of this book, I send my sincerest love to Joshua Beckman; Rob Schlegel; Zachary Schomburg; Neil Harris and Kelly Shimoda; Elisabeth Benjamin, Lucas Farrell and Molly McDonald; and Lisa Schumaier ...